Paleo Smoothies:

Paleo Smoothie Recipes For Weight Loss

By

Valerie Alston

Table of Contents

Paleo Smoothies: Paleo Smoothie Recipes For Weight Loss

By Valerie Alston

First Published, 2014

Printed in the United States of America

Introduction

The Paleo diet assumes eating foods and drinking beverages that are at their most natural forms. Paleo is short for Palaeolithic; it is the era where our early ancestors appeared on earth. This diet therefore follows what a Paleolithic man ate: freshly caught fish, game and meats, eggs, fruits and vegetables. There is no room for food additives, flavorings and chemicals to preserve food. Proponents of the Paleo diet believe that by following what our ancient ancestors ate, we will also be able to achieve healthy and strong bodies like what a Paleolithic man had.

Paleo smoothies are delicious smoothies made from fruits, vegetables and herbs that may be eaten in a Paleo diet plan. Smoothies are very common in a Paleo diet meal plan since this is one of the easiest ways to take in fruits, vegetables and herbs. We all know that these foods contain numerous nutrients that are very important in keeping the body healthy and thus these should be taken in adequate amounts in a Paleo diet. And a part from smoothies being an easy and practical way to take in nutrients, it is also fun to drink smoothies. Even small children will love to drink ice cold smoothies as desserts or for a snack; definitely this is a great way to sneak in nutrients in your kids' diets.

Paleo smoothies to lose weight

Aside from having a lot of vitamins and minerals, fruits and veggies also contain natural properties that are beneficial to weight loss. One of these is fiber. Fiber in fruits and vegetables are difficult to digest and therefore these stay longer in the gastrointestinal system. Fiber acts like brooms that sweep the colon clean from toxins, chemical and microorganisms that may cause illness. And as fiber is difficult to digest, it stays in the stomach longer and hence you do not feel the urge to eat in between meals anymore. And of course the cleaner your colon is the more regular your bowel movement is which will help you feel better in the long run.

Preparing Paleo diet smoothies

In preparing most Paleo diet smoothies, you need a few important kitchen equipment. First you need a reliable multispeed blender so you can blend different kinds of fruits and vegetables. Your blender should have removable blade attachments so you can also use if to crush ice. Your blender should also be easy to clean and maintain as well. Another great kitchen appliance, but not really a necessity in smoothies preparation, is a juicer.

A juicer is a small machine that can turn a whole fruit or a whole vegetable into juice. From the skin or the pulp of the fruit or the vegetable down to the meat, it's a guarantee that you will be able to get all the nutrients from these foods in no time at all. Juicing herbs are another thing since herbs are finer to juice up. A special juicer called a masticating juice will cold press fruits and vegetables as well as herbs. Choosing the ideal juicer and blender will help you create the most nutritious and the most flavorful smoothies at home. And with using blenders and juicers, you will also be able to make glasses upon glasses of smoothies for weight loss for you and your family.

Paleo smoothies recipes for weight loss

In this book you will find a collection of smoothies that follow a Paleo diet plan which are perfect for weight loss. All the ingredients mentioned here are standard but you may increase the amounts of each to be able to make Paleo diet smoothies for everyone. Be sure to use only the freshest and possibly organic fruits and veggies for your diet smoothies.

Thick Banana Smoothie

This is a smoothies recipe that uses ripe bananas. There are a lot of nutrients in bananas and possibly the most important is potassium. Potassium regulates the cardiovascular system and is also important in many metabolic functions of the body. In this recipe, you will need about one large ripe banana, half a cup of cold coconut milk, a cup of cashew butter, 2 pitted dates, a teaspoon of maple syrup (you may adjust the amount of maple syrup according to your taste. You may add a teaspoon more if you think this is too bland), a pinch of sea salt and a cup of crushed ice.

Cut the bananas into small pieces if you are using a blender but if you are using a juicer you may already place a whole, peeled banana in the juicer. Blend this very well and then add the coconut milk, cashew butter and dates. Add the salt and then the amount of maple syrup that you wish. Blend this for half a minute or until the dates have been completely processed and mixed. Place the crushed ice next and then pulse for 5 seconds. You may serve this at once or serve later by placing the mixture in the refrigerator.

Tropical Strawberry Smoothie Recipe

Coconut and strawberries make a perfect tropical/berry smoothie. Coconut has a lot of antioxidants and nutrients while strawberries are a rich source of vitamin C. You will need 250 ml of fresh coconut milk, about 10 frozen strawberries (frozen berries are perfect in making the smoothie drink cold and thick), about 3 fresh strawberries, a teaspoon of almond butter, a tablespoon of fresh coconut meat shavings and a teaspoon of honey (again you may add more honey to make the smoothie sweeter or do without using hone at all especially for diabetics).

Remove strawberries from the freezer only when you are about to use them. Place berries in a blender and then pulse for about half a minute. Add the milk and butter and blend until all the ingredients have been completely mixed. Add the honey and then continue to pulse for about 5 seconds. Pour the contents in a tall glass, garnish it with coconut shavings and sliced strawberries.

Raspberry and Mint Smoothie

Raspberries contain a lot of vitamins and minerals which are perfect for improving immunity. Mint is an herb that is rich in vitamin C and minerals such as potassium, copper and calcium. This recipe needs about 5 fresh mint leaves, 1 ½ cups of raspberries (preferably frozen), a tablespoon of coconut or maple syrup, half a cup of chilled orange juice and a cup of crushed ice.

Prepare the leaves by making sure these are clean before you place in a juicer or a blender and wash the raspberries thoroughly. Blend the raspberries; add the mint leaves and then the orange juice. Blend these ingredients for about half a minute and then place the coconut syrup in the mixture and continue to blend for another minute. Finally, add the crushed ice and then pulse for another 5 seconds. Place the mixture in a tall glass and garnish with raspberries and a mint leaf on top of the glass. You may also place this in a ready-to-go glass container with a straw so you can drink your smoothies even when you are outdoors.

Watermelon Honey Lemon Smoothie

Watermelons are considered one of the healthiest foods in the world because it is high in lycopene which is important for a healthy cardiovascular system. The fruit is also rich in vitamin C, pantothenic acid, copper, biotin and vitamin A to name a few. When combined with honey and lemon, you get a smoothie that delivers a complete supply of vitamins and minerals that they body needs to be healthy each day. For this watermelon honey lemon smoothie you will need About 2 cups of watermelons, juice of one lime, a teaspoon of honey and a cup of crushed ice.

Prepare the watermelon by slicing it and removing the tough skin. Be sure to slice really close to the skin since this is where nutrients are mostly found. Chop into small pieces so you can easily blend them. Place in a blender and then add the lime and honey. When the mixture is smooth, add the crushed ice and blend for another 10 seconds. Place the mixture in a tall glass or in a covered beverage container so you can take it to work or as you commute.

Coffee Choco and Banana Smoothie

As mentioned bananas contain a lot of vitamins and minerals which are mostly important in cardiovascular health. Cocoa and coffee are rich sources of antioxidants which are ideal in reducing the risk of cardiovascular diseases, reducing the effects of aging and a so many more. This is a very thick choco and coffee smoothie and you will need a medium sized ripe banana, 3 pitted dried dates, about 1/3 cup of hazelnuts, a teaspoon of honey (you may increase or decrease the amount of honey according to your taste, a tablespoon of cocoa powder, ¼ cup of espresso coffee, a cup of almond milk and crushed ice.

Remove banana peel and then slice bananas into smaller pieces. Blend bananas, dried dates, nuts, milk and honey. When the mixture is thick, add the coffee and then pulse for about 10 more seconds. Finally, add the crushed ice and then mix for another 5 seconds and then serve. This smoothie recipe serves 2; double the ingredients to make 4 or more servings. Espresso coffee could make the recipe taste bitter and so you may add or reduce honey as you wish.

Fruits and Greens Smoothie

Unlike the previous recipes, this one uses vegetables as ingredients. If you have never tried a veggie smoothie before then this is a great starter since it is not too sweet and too bitter too. You will need a small head of organic lettuce, a large bunch of organic spinach, about 3 stalks of celery, an organic apple, an organic ripe pear and a whole organic banana. You will also need about 1 ½ cups of water and the juice of ½ lemon. Optional ingredients include coriander stems and parsley stems.

Wash the vegetables first in running water before placing them in a blender or food processor. Add water and the lemon juice and continue to mix until you get a smooth consistency. Chop the apples, pears and bananas just before placing these in a blender. Add the optional ingredients last. If the mixture is too strong or too bland for you, you may add a teaspoon of honey. Finally, add crushed ice and then continue to blend. This recipe is very flexible since you can reduce or double the ingredients as you wish.

The Green Wellness Smoothie

If you prefer a sweeter and much more tolerable green Paleo smoothie then this is the recipe for you. This is a sweeter because of adding coconut water and more fruits; greens included in this recipe will provide you great amounts of fiber and nutrients that you will need to start your day. There are also live good bacteria ingredients in this recipe to help improve your immune system. You will need about 3 medium size stalks of kale (use only the leaves, choose fresh leaves and discard large wilting ones), 3 large cos lettuce leaves, a cup of coconut water, a small whole ripe banana, a handful of gogi berries or you may use blueberries, a cup of hemp seeds, a teaspoon of chia seeds, a teaspoon of maca powder, a teaspoon of honey and a teaspoon of spirulina.

Clean the green veggies you will need for this recipe, remove banana peel and chop bananas into small pieces and wash the berries. Place all the ingredients in a blender and then blend for about half a minute. Add the hemp seeds, coconut water and chia seeds and then pulse for about 5 more minutes. Add honey and maca powder, mix for another 5 minutes and then finally add the spirulina. Mix the ingredients thoroughly. You may add crushed ice if you wish or pour the mixture in a tall glass with two ice cubes and serve.

A Green Power-Up Smoothie

If you feel very tired even upon waking up in the morning then this smoothie recipe is the best way to wake and power you up. Ingredients found in this recipe contain high amounts of iodine, vitamin D and antioxidants. You may also drink this in the middle of the day when you feel low in energy. You will need a cup of fresh coconut water, a cup of oats milk, a tablespoon of coconut oil, a tablespoon of flaxseed meal, a teaspoon of spirulina, a half cup of frozen berries (blueberries, Gogi berries, strawberries or blackberries will do as long as these are frozen overnight), a teaspoon of probiotics, 2 tablespoons of natural yoghurt, a dash of cinnamon and 2 drops of stevia.

Wash the berries before freezing them overnight. Place the coconut oil, flaxseed meal, coconut water, and yoghurt in the blender and mix. Add the berries, cinnamon and stevia and mix for another 10 seconds. Finally add the spirulina and probiotics and then mix really well for another 10 seconds. You may add crushed ice if you wish but usually the frozen berries would suffice.

Detoxifying Green Smoothie

Every day that passes by the body becomes toxic with chemicals, pollution and harmful microorganisms and the most important way to remove toxins is to go on a cleansing diet. This smoothie recipe will help cleanse the body and provide energy that you need for the morning. You will need a small bunch of English spinach, a small handful of fresh mint leaves, a handful of fresh parsley, a tablespoon of lemon juice, a small cucumber, three or four medium size lettuce leaves, a few stalks of celery and about 3 cm of fresh ginger. You will also need crushed ice or about 5 ice cubes.

Prepare the vegetables by washing them. Cut the cucumber lengthwise in small pieces and then peel the ginger and slice it into small lengthwise pieces. Blend the veggies together in a blender until you get a smooth mixture. Add lemon juice and then blend the mixture for another 5 seconds. Add crushed ice and then pulse or you may pour the ingredients in a tall glass with ice cubes.

Mixed Berries with Fresh Orange Juice Smoothie

Berries and oranges provide a great source of vitamin C which is known to improve the body's ability to fight diseases, improve skin and hair health, increase the body's immunity and will also help fight aging. You will need a pack of mixed frozen berries or if you wish you could use one kind of berry at a time (favorite berries include, blueberries, strawberries and blackberries), a medium size ripe banana, a large orange and half a cup of pomegranate juice.

You need to wash berries before keeping them in the deep freeze overnight. Remove the banana peel and slice the banana into small pieces, slice the oranges into small pieces. Place the fruits and pomegranate juice in a blender and then mix thoroughly. You may add crushed ice and blend for another 10 seconds. Serve in a tall glass with chunks of strawberries on top or an orange piece as a decoration.

Power-Up Creamy Mango Smoothie

This is a deliciously sweet smoothie because it is made from ripe ingredients. Mangoes and avocados are two of the best foods that have amazing amounts of vitamins and minerals. You will need 1 ripe avocado, 2 medium size ripe mangoes, and a cup of freshly squeezed orange juice and a cup of water. You may also place crushed ice if you wish instead of water.

Place the mangoes in the deep freeze overnight and scoop these from the skin when you are ready to prepare your smoothie. Cut the avocado in half and remove the huge seed, remove the peel and cut into small pieces. Place these in the blender and then mix until you get a smooth consistency. Add the orange juice and then blend for another 5 seconds and then add crushed ice or water. Place the mixture in a tall glass; this recipe makes about two tall glasses of creamy smoothies.

Fruit Medley Smoothies

Fruits will perk you up in the morning and will provide the body's needed nutrients. You can make smoothies from any kind of fruit but the sweeter the better. For a sweet fruit medley you will need about 2 cups of fresh pineapple juice, 2 cups of fresh strawberries, a medium size ripe banana, a medium size mango and a medium size peach.

Place slices of pineapple in a juicer to yield fresh pineapple juice. Wash strawberries and other fruits before slicing them. Peel and cut the banana into small pieces, dice the mangoes and then dice the peaches. Place the ingredients in a blender as well as the freshly squeezed pineapple juice. Blend these until you get a smooth consistency. You may also place crushed ice when the mixture is smooth and blend for another 5 seconds.

Naturally Sweet Paleo Fruit Smoothie

Green smoothies are good for you but it may look unappetizing and taste bland this is why people new to Paleo smoothies should first try a naturally sweet fruit smoothie. You will need a medium size ripe avocado, a small ripe pear, a medium size ripe banana, freshly squeezed ripe pineapple juice or lemon juice and a teaspoon of raw honey. You may also add crushed ice.

It's best if you freeze all the fruit ingredients before preparing them if you do not want to use crushed ice. Process the pineapple or simply place slices in a juicer to yield fresh pineapple juice. Remove the peel of the avocado and then slice into small pieces, remove the peel of the pear and then slice and remove the peel of the ripe banana and slice into smaller pieces. Place all these in a blender along with the pineapple juice and blend until you get a smooth consistency. Add the raw honey and the crushed ice last and then pulse for another 5 seconds. Serve in tall glasses.

Red, Yellow and Orange Smoothie

Smoothies are great for kids since it is colourful and cold. Kids will love to drink smoothies every day because of these reasons and little do they know, it is also the best way for parents to sneak in nutrients that they need to stay healthy each day. You will need a small carrot, a medium size ripe apple, a pear, a medium size orange, a cup of frozen strawberries, a cup of orange juice and a cup of ice cubes.

Scrub the carrot and then cut into small pieces with the peel intact. Wash, peel and core the apple. Peel and then slice the pear into small pieces and peel the oranges. Wash the strawberries before storing them in the deep freeze. Place all the chopped fruits and the berries in a blender and then blend until you get a smooth consistency. Add the orange juice last and then blend the mixture for another 5 seconds. Pour this in a tall glass with ice in it and then serve immediately. You may also use crushed ice; just place this along with the orange juice.

A Summer Fruity Smoothie Recipe

Summer's hot temperature will easily leave you dehydrated and this recipe is perfect for replenishing the fluids and minerals lost from the heat. You will need a ½ cup of cantaloupe, a ½ cup of pineapple, a ½ cup of cranberry juice, 1/3 cup of sliced ripe banana, ¼ cup of pineapple juice, a tablespoon of honey, ¾ teaspoon of lemon juice.

Cut the fruits into smaller pieces and place in a blender. Mix these completely along with a cup of crushed ice, pineapple juice, lemon juice and honey. You may use additional honey to make the recipe sweeter but naturally using ripe fruits will suffice. You can omit the crushed ice if you wish and just pour the mixture in a tall glass with ice cubes.

Thick Fruity Smoothies with Fresh Strawberries

Another fruity smoothie version but this recipe is different with coconut oil, coconut flour and honey. You will get a sweet thick mixture similar to a pudding. Fruits included in this recipe are all ripe so you will get an extra ordinarily sweet mix. You will need about 3 tablespoons of coconut oil (coconut oil is waxy in room temperature so place this in a warm water bath to melt it gently), a tablespoon of coconut flour, 2 tablespoons of honey, a large ripe banana, a cup of pineapple chunks, a cup of fresh strawberries, 2 kiwis, a large ripe mango and a cup of crushed ice.

Prepare the fruits by peeling them and slicing them into small pieces. Mash the banana in a small bowl. Set the fruits aside. Combine the coconut oil and the coconut flour in a small bowl; mix these to get a thick consistency. Add the honey and the mashed banana. Place this mixture in a blender and then mix for about 10 seconds. Add the fresh fruits and the juices and mix completely. Add the crushed ice last. Some may dislike a very rich consistency and so you may add a teaspoon of water at a time until you get a smoother consistency.

Delicious Kale Smoothie Shake

Kales are the most unlikely vegetable you will choose as a smoothie but it is very popular since kale is a vegetable with very low cholesterol, high fiber content and has great amounts of protein, riboflavin and thiamine. For this kale smoothie recipe you will need 4 stalks of kale, 4 stems of celery, a cucumber, a medium-size pear, ½ ginger and crushed ice or a cup of water.

Wash kale leaves carefully along with the celery stems. Cut the cucumber into small pieces and peel the pear and cut these into smaller pieces too. Peel the ginger. Place all these ingredients in a blender and mix until you get a smooth consistency. Add the crushed ice last and if you think that the mixture is too bland, you may add a teaspoon of raw honey.

Protein Kale and Coconut Smoothie

This is a perfect fruit and protein smoothie that will power up your day; you must drink this protein shake during breakfast so you will have vitamins and minerals to begin your day and protein for energy. You will need a cup or two of water, a cup of blueberries, 3 stalks of kale, half a cup of shredded coconut, a tablespoon of chlorella, one to two scoops of protein powder (whey or casein will do).

Wash the blueberries and then place these in a blender along with the kale, shredded coconut and chlorella. Mix these until you get a smooth consistency. Add the protein powder and water (the amount of water that you add may depend on the thickness of the mixture that you want).

Final Words

You can absolutely use Paleo smoothies to reduce weight on a regular basis. You can drink smoothies during breakfast when you need a huge energy boost or during an afternoon snack. You can even make your own smoothie just be sure that you stick to the Paleo principle: no processed ingredients and if possible and keep the ingredients as simple and as fresh or organic as you can.

Paleo smoothies for weight loss should also be used along with the right diet plan, an efficient exercise routine and lifestyle change to be able to totally keep of the weight that you lost for good. You may find drinking paleo smoothies different from drinking the usual sweet smoothies variety simply because it lacks the flavour that you are used to. What you can do is to use natural flavors like honey, bee pollen, coconut water or ripe fruits to compensate with the taste. If possible, do not add artificial sweeteners as well since these are still processed chemicals that should be avoided in a Paleo diet plan.

I want to personally thank you for reading my book. I hope you found information in this book useful and I would be very grateful if you could leave your honest review about this book. I certainly want to thank you in advance for doing this.